THE
SUBLIMATION
OF FREDERICK
ECKERT

THE
SUBLIMATION
OF FREDERICK
ECKERT

TRAVIS
CEBULA

Black
Lawrence
Press

Black
Lawrence
Press

www.blacklawrence.com

Executive Editor: Diane Goettel
Book and cover design: Amy Freels
Cover art: "Diving Board" by Travis Cebula

Published 2017 by Black Lawrence Press.
Printed in the United States.

Contents

Part 3: Epilogue

For Shannon

A great feat of engineering is an object of perpetual interest to people bent on self-destruction. Since its completion, the Empire State Building, a gigantic shard of the Hoosier State torn from the mild limestone bosom of the Midwest and upended, on the site of the old Waldorf-Astoria, in the midst of the heaviest traffic in the world, had been a magnet for dislocated souls hoping to ensure the finality of their impact, or to mock the bold productions of human vanity.

—Michael Chabon, *The Amazing Adventures of Kavalier & Clay*

No one sleeps in the sky. No one.
—Federico García Lorca, *Poet in New York*

PART 1: PRECIPITATION

LEAPS TO HIS DEATH OFF EMPIRE TOWER

Unidentified Man Eludes Guard and Plunges From Stairway Above 102d Floor Observatory.

VISITORS SEE THE TRAGEDY

German Postcards in Pocket Sole Clue to Identity of First to Leap Off Building.

An unidentified man got past a guard stationed on the staircase leading from the 102d-floor observatory of the Empire State Building to the top floor yesterday, hurdled a four-foot circular wall and leaped to his death. His body hurtled past the eighty-eighth-floor observatory in view of twenty visitors and landed on the roof of a promenade on the eighty-sixth floor.

The victim was about 35 years old, five feet seven inches tall, weighed about 145 pounds, and had blond hair and blue eyes. From a signature attached to a postal card which was found in a pocket of his gray suit, which was of German manufacture, his name was believed to be Frederich Eckert. The card, a group photograph of several German school boys and a priest, was unaddressed and undated. Written on the reverse side in German were the following words:

"My darling: This is a picture of my son, Arnim, which was taken in Astoria, L. I., June 4, 1930."

Two other photographs, a German prayer book, two religious medals, $5.52 and a small package of cigars were also found in his pockets by the police. The photographs, one of a young German boy and the other of a woman and a boy, also bore German writing on their reverse sides.

The man's nervousness was so apparent as he rode up in the elevator from the eighty-sixth floor to the topmost observatory on the 102d floor that he attracted the attention of Pierrepont L. Stackpole of Boston, another passenger. Throughout the short ride, Stackpole said, the man nervously fingered five cigars which he carried in a small package.

When the elevator operator opened the door to the glass-enclosed observation tower, the man darted out and vaulted an iron gate in front of the stairway leading to an open landing on the 103d floor, which was intended for the use of passengers disembarking from airships. Robert Andry of 305 Haven Avenue, Washington Heights, a guard, started after the man but was unable to catch him.

Before landing on the eighty-sixth floor, the body struck the base of the mooring mast, breaking some glass. From there it fell to the roof of the promenade without attracting the attention of diners in a near-by restaurant.

The leap was the first suicide since the building, the tallest in the world, was opened to the public. Prior to the official opening, however, a discharged workman jumped down an elevator shaft from the top of the structure and landed on the eightieth floor.

3

PART 2: THE SUBLIMATION OF FREDERICK ECKERT

Hypothesis

what if

every ledge provided only   [what if]
an opportunity to choose—

whether to approach   [now]
quickly, or hesitatingly.
and if.
and if at the end

the faith nestled in
each line was an edge—   [we agreed to]
would you
linger or   [leap into]

                                                    [   ]

more or less to
note the lack of sound—

in anticipation
silence congeals

on the audience as they
continue

to wait for a human form
to enter the sky.

Catalyst for Ordination #1

it has been said
that in a vacuum—
which is to say,
a space without breath or   [without a little]
wind in it—
feathers and rocks
will fall, like humans,
at exactly the same rate.

and those who saw
it happen, they said   [a little]
he fell like a spider—
something about the limbs,

they said, and they said   [a little]

the word, "carom"—
as if it applied to a human—

and manifest in that word
was the exact historic mixture
of hard sounds
battering soft—

and how beautiful,
his vestment fluttered—   [a little]

and what if—

if he survived?
would we—

recognize him   [a little more]

by his limping?

Catechism

where is the wind?

there are 103 floors to climb.   [be patient]

here is a chrome door.
there is sunlight nearer.
here is a narrow flight
of stairs.
there are four steps
between the stairs and the sky   [be assured]

here is the puff of his breath.
there is fog, briefly.
here is a drowsy guard.
there is a wall, knee high,   [have faith]
made of grey stone.

there is the wind,   [we have]
wind cold enough to cut
granite.   [prayer]

and gravity
four steps forward. one up.
and there
he's gone. Our Father   [and we]
who   [still]
art in Heaven.   [breathe]

in the myth

out there.
there is the wind.

Catalyst for Confirmation #1

a subway door hisses open.

memories are a local train—
inside of a dog,
the dreaming that goes on
inside of a dog or   [the smell]
inside of a downtown car,
the old man is sleeping.
the numbers count out Brooklyn
bound and down.   [or the feel of]
getting smaller.   [almost like trees]

it would be a mistake
to assume it was because he was old—   [and given texture]
or only because—
that the man wrapped himself
in the consecrated skin that lines
the gut of the City, or that he
trapped himself unwillingly on
the various tines of fiberglass,   [not wood, but]
bucket chairs, sliding doors, stainless
steel, windows, and vinyl veneer.   [something]
hard and screwed into a wall.
walnut. the color of walnut. the grain.
he chose this raiment, as much as
he chose life in the masses—

a graffiti-strewn coffin—like motion, like

any of us choose our own container of sleep.   [from which to
                                                        build]

in fact, he could have immolated himself
in pollen, chosen a rural life and a puff
of yellow smoke   [a more resilient pew]
rising from a meadow. and, in fact—
once, he did. but not now.
this *now* of his flowers into injection-
molded plastic and smells like amnesia.   [or anesthesia]
it would be a mistake to assume it was
because he was young—   [this]
or only because—he tied hemp
twine around his finger.   [it fills]
but he was young, then, and not now.
this man is.   [a tin plate]
this man was.
this man could have been
this man as easily as any other.

he coughs into a blue
scrap of t-shirt. a door closes.   [with]

side tunnels of if and if and if.   [smoke]
diminishing. he remembers nothing
below 14th street. he remembers nothing
below 8th, nothing

below Houston, and when the train reaches
the broad gap of Canal, he wakes—   [hangs in the air for a
                                                         moment]
and remembers. if if. if, if. if.
nothing there, too. the dog goes on dreaming
in the shade of a linden tree. to be a dog in
Central Park at noon in November and   [like a grey curtain]
a warm hand on your head. what could be
better? the old man's image of the girl begins   [like velvet]

and ends at 4th street, the one he thinks of   [curtains]
as she, and only as she, and nameless,   [and stony]
and 4th where it defines Washington Square—   [rood screen]
its little corner that always connected   [waiting with]
dirt and heroin and the unwashed young until—

a door opens. a door hisses closed.
the City drapes herself in the sun's
raiment—miter, autumn and all.
and all falls hissing into the Hudson.

until when? maybe he should have asked for her name, or
listened, then. to have more than *she*—one name more
than the one he suffers.
a new one. she seemed afraid,
held her happy dog on its short leash,
its feathered tail waving back and forth.
rhythmic. like a ride out on Coney,   [hope]
like a lightbulb screwed into every surface,   [and a prayer]
you could make out
silhouettes coloring midnight.

he never saw her again.
or rather, he saw her everywhere, but
she wasn't her—
and there was no grass, only granite   [with]
the hot glare of the sun on
a triumphal arch. and thus irony. and noontide.
he had only asked her to dance, innocent,
once with him in the open air. she declined, refined [penitence]
to the end, that one, and beautiful
in a scarf and a pounded felt hat, that purple
he thought, always looked pounded.
and a boy always looked—

his head pounding, against the window,
the clacking of wheels intrudes on sleep. asleep

under the financial district and nearing the end—   [to
                                    proclaim faithfulness]

he swore to her as he rounded the black
stone pew, in his hardest voice he swore to her
and that damned hat and City and dog and any   [eternal]
addicts sitting still long enough to listen
in Washington Square on a Sunday,
he swore that he would come back.   [and everlasting]
mark him, mark the calendar, mark
the clock's face with tattoos
and the tolling of bells.   [to the faithless]
the world would end when
he stopped coming back.

a door hisses open. the masses stand.

he would be back, and back, and back,
every day until she married him and if not   [he believed]
he'd marry the City, by god, the City herself,   [in]
that terrible and huge and frightening bucket
that could hold him and her and her scarf and that
stupid pounded hat and dogs and garbage and everything.
                                        [beauty]
and everything. he never saw
her again. he was old then, and suddenly, and true
to his word, he married the City anyway   [she was so
                                    beautiful]

and he figured it wasn't her fault, it was less than   [that]
her fault and the girl was probably
a terrible dancer anyway, what with that scarf   [he]

15

and everything and anyway the City—
fuck, the City was a nightmare
but   [unwittingly]
he chose her, he had every chance to leave but   [committed]

he married her and worshipped her
and found himself on his knees more   [himself]
than once, heaven knows. and so, they clung   [to a life]
together, he and his City, all clung and cozy
in a walk-up on the Lower East Side, at least
at night. and *anyway* was there as the third wheel.   [of concrete
                                                    and glass towers]

at least until they got divorced

or she left, or anyway the City seemed to,   [to forget flowers]
she seemed to recede, to be bereft, and he was alone   [to forget]
and old, then, too. and elsewhere,   [reinforced]
the dog kept on dreaming
of an old man on a train and didn't ask why,   [to forget why]
he just watched him sleep, felt his breath escape   [and happily]
in visible puffs of cheap gin. and the old

door hisses back open, just like the lid
of the world rolled sideways, yawns, and the old

man pounds his dreams of the girl in the purple
hat into himself. his fists curl and the City tucks   [the width of]
her dreams of them all under her arm.
and the City slept below herself. and in spite of.
almost as if she believed in them, too.   [the sky]
and, in her way, the City confirmed
that they lived—the born, sleeping, risen dead, the   [cloudless
                                                        sky]

dog, girl, man, subway.

confirmed their limbs and minds were firm   [and starry]
for a while before the end. the end of the downtown
line approaches, and under the East River   [black like]
the old man breathes.
the dog thinks belief is like that.
like breathing under a river.   [a river plummets]

the masses sit. the door hisses—
open. just one more time.

she relaxes one warm hand onto
his forehead, and with the other
adjusts her hat just so
she can lean lower and linger   [into the sun]
there—*love you, you know. I've always
loved you.*   [and happily]

Catalyst for Baptism #1

easier than a face,
he decides to imagine the girl   [like]
a name,
thin as it is, to wear   [the secret]
as her own sacred raiment—
a ribbon, say—   [name]
say, for her hair, for her,
so he can distinguish her
from the masses in his head.

so he can say her,   [for god]

he goes to the shrinking closet
in his head where he stores
the names of everything he's
ever named. he doesn't remember
who wore most of the names, or what,

like he doesn't recall who wore   [or]
the books or hats or glasses—

calmly, he forgets,   [the deep incantations]
especially the ones at the back
of the closet or the front, and so—   [required]

when he pulls a name from the hook
next to where he keeps his own,
he only almost recognizes it.

he squeezes his eyes
shut, so the answer will
be a surprise. opens them—
opens his chest, his chest opens,
exhales, and his mouth speaks—   [for flight]

and when it speaks it says, *Carole.*

Catalyst for First Communion #1

[if I forgot my son. as if to not remember me.
as if to not eat would be the same as
to take this. take all this and eat it.
the same as. as if an exit was
bread. as if breaking bread was.
as if to celebrate was a
harvest. as if the broken
would fall to fallow then.
and then we would.
and then gather them in
as if to exit. this field of wheat.
it sits. as if it waits for rupture—
passively—which is to say, as if
it shall resist departure,
and if we ever leave it, it shall persist.
as if none of us ever meant to. as if we
never left. the City shall be
and it shall be as if
we shall return.
and we are going, as if more to a mass
than an arrival—
as if to a departure, rather.
as if to exit]

was,   in that moment,   love.
as if afflicted,
he ate. he ate it all.   all that was offered,
and it blistered his throat.

the feast was so   hot.
all were ever so—

and he would do the same   again.
he prayed to everything.
anyone might have.   the masses do—

we will give away   our breath.
amen.
and we will offer up   our lives
at this table.

amen.
give us someone to sit next to,
amen,
they pray,   and *we will honor them.*
give us all this creation,   please,   these
grease-stains on paper plates,
this opulence of oranges,
and social nuance.

give us a slice fat enough to roll.
give us old love   and thin napkins.
please, they pray,   *please,* they pray
to the other, to Spring Street, to Famous Ben's—
they pray.   they pray to each
red vinyl chair and each chrome leg—
to the strange *we* that forms inside

a fluorescent box. steam clings to
a glass door, to linoleum.   it stands
between the yellow cabs,   handsome,
like a Lincoln slick with rain crawls
up Thompson Street   between
the black doors.

so we walk out   and we straighten our
backs.
so we feast on our dead selves.
we hold wakes.
we eat to honor our dead,
so black in the presence of our living,
beautiful eyes.   we dye the world
onto the foreheads of horses in such a
way that ostrich plumes
and chips of obsidian,
are, in their way, less   rare.
like letters,

black jewels   linger in a bookstore.
resplendent sidewalks
are clad in black, too,   and the canticle
the masses walk into—those others
who put on their best clothes
only when they go out. the masses.
the masses celebrate a life
less aimless,
and more. they write   their wisdom
on the walls of subways—

get more comfortable with time, its sacrifice, and
its chewing.
they say   *things get easier after that.*
the first bite is hard, but kneel
and you will get
to feast on the bones of strangers.

we are buried in them.
if not yet, we find a way to be.
if not,   then we dissolve
into the same ground our grandparents did.

if we are lucky, we grow
before that, and will again. and amen.

this City, she has swallowed
more than just us,   and moreover,
we will all be breathed again.
if you can stand it,   then stand
in this air,   it has been breathed and may
be the sigh of faith
as it escapes—if you can stand
with the supplicants, you are weft

with the masses in paupers' gowns.
the masses multiply
into others.   the gloaming
other may be other
than flesh.   share such that
I am the sea, too, made into
the flesh of your flesh.
of you,   it is faces.

take this air, each
from your own body.
it. it is the breath   and faces of
each of you.   breathe
trust—take this air,
this raiment, this holy robe—
clad yourself in sacred purple. amen.

in the masses
blooms a heaviness—
a sacrament, breath—
the holy mass of it.

Catalyst for Ordination #2

he went happily to nothing.

it was his own casualty that stopped him.
but it was 1932 and hard to be
Frederick Eckert, who, as Frederick Eckert,
had tipped just past enough. he went. he went   [outside]
rough with a German prayer book and two
religious medallions in his pocket,
one each for his widening eyes. they said—

if Icarus were given leaves
of the Bible, it would have ended
the same as feathers—

whether it was morning or not, it was   [the cathedral]
the Great Depression, they said,
in the Empire, it was
November 3rd and the 103rd
floor. so the sun was low as he sprinted—
altitude and winter being what they are—
out of the elevator, past the drowsy
guards and at last over the rood
screen that divided building from sky.

and drafted the curve of gravity a-
cross the angels' stair.

like gemstones or sunlight,
his path would have become vertical—   [a line]
but for the wind—but it was decided, then,
at the last, he would swerve

into a falcon's perspective—life in death,   [of holy]
hunger, hunger for the hard
earth and other birds, a wordless call to tell

the narrow world all he saw on the way
down—the glass, the walls, the
rivers, the water towers, the   [pilgrims]
stones, the bricks, the steel, the
pigeons in their fear, the black talons,   [begged for]
the flowers, the poor huddled

trees, the maples, the bees, the concrete, the
garbage, the antennas, the ropes,
the wires that competed with wires, the
taxis, the umbrellas, and the masses—   [his return]

so beautiful, he whispered as
his arms strained backwards into
blue tendons and sky, *bless me*

and make me beautiful, too, make me
a grey wing and let the wind
eat me whole.   [before returning]

I will whistle through the fall.
I will tug the wind through
the street itself, through
the park's slats and benches.   [to the ground]

so the City she blessed him;   [before he shattered]
just let the building kiss him.   [they begged]

Catalyst for Confirmation #2

alone with his   questions,
and *aren't we*—
all—

aren't we meant?
to question distance

he queried the sky
whether it had always been
deeper at its center—

how far away
the indigo—

looks

on faces,

in waves, and smaller,
the distance   between
being a young
man and being   an old man
dwindles into
minutiae—

a distance
walked—
a meal
not eaten.

a grey beard
full of scrambled
eggs—

I blink more than
I used to.
I see less of—

the shrinkage   of his right—
his eye and the growth of
hunger   trade stories
over a distance from
hunger.   a thirst overcomes

him—
is this myself?
am I?
within this   sack of skin—
still. unmoving.
he asks and asks—
when was I young?
then—

five unlit cigars and five fingers—

a hand.

was that   faith?

then—

can I write this   down?

then—

this coming
down—

this if—

this descent—

Eucharist

to ash
finally

and

.

to breath

binds itself
breath

respiration

as by

an unanswered

question
is

survival

Catalyst for Baptism #2

before a storm.
closed into   stillness—

and too quickly—

the sky, until scolded—
glows—brief as

pleasant dreams   on the uptown train.

an old man, this
Frederick Eckert, floats—
into bloom—for once, he is
quiet as a narcissus beginning   its
one warm day in February—

the dwindling   wind   on

his closed eyes—

the soft sun.   chrome poles dance.
a gull sleeps   on the sea.

like gravestones or
snow—
mud is the memory, too, of
a five-year-old boy in
another winter   gone—

Catalyst for Confirmation #3

him
and happily then

in the sun

a river that plummets

black like

and starry

the cloudless sky

same the sky

same the width of

a church and happily
forget

reinforced
to forget
to forget flowers

of concrete and glass
grey

to the same life
himself

committed
unwillingly

he

that

she was so beautiful

beauty

in that
he believed

for the faithless

and everlasting

for eternally

to proclaim faithfulness

for the other

fires

and flame

waits with
its rude screen
and stony
curtains to

lick velvet

grey

hangs in the air for a
moment—

smoke—
the slippers of burnt
sandalwood—

until

with stale incense

until with smoke
it

fills a tin plate

this
anesthesia

a more lasting pew

from which to build

something

not wood, but

flame

and if given something
to burn—

Catalyst for Confirmation #4

the city is concrete, yes, but   concrete
I can't describe, like feelings.
like love,   I only have examples
to prove it's there—

turtle pond the turtle pond—
I prefer to be with you on a quiet
night.   I prefer to be with you when   everything
is stripped bare   like rapture.

Catalyst for Extreme Unction #1

the water bathes his face.   [the remnants of]
last night's downpours gurgle into
a storm drain, a medium for the swimming
forms of a paper plate and polystyrene   [life in a]
clamshell. the plate snags on the bars
of a cast-iron grate, and the rain
flows past with other trash and mistakes.   [broken]
a few puddles remain, shrivel,
as trapped as the plate, as coated with
grease. in the dream, a memory of food.   [bed]
beneath the old man, the City is dreaming.
the masses beneath the rain are a little cleaner.   [bloom]

he forgives them for this.

he has nowhere better.

from his Grand Terminal pew,
the old man treads water
under the blanket of his dream.
daylight gnaws at something that might have been
Sunday, or clouds, if not for the wind.
if not for the wind he might still be
inside and dreaming. but this.   [in]

this is a return to the slow digestion

of alms outside the station. and without
marking the time he has begun   [raw]
waiting again. he forgets the improbable
chain of causation, his interior narration   [flowers]
punctuated with profanity and the fear-
laced dregs of sanity. he forgets his
name when he hands his story to the City.
take it, he thinks, *I don't need or want*
this dream anymore. it is a bad dream—   [flowers and a sore]

only—. one dirty quarter appears in
his palm in return. *this is to pay for*
the ticket out, he knows. at the bottom of
every bottle is a ticket and then he will be forgiven,
too. one long bottle of forgiven while he dreams
of the subway that will take him home.
he tries to remember his home, and can't.   [without a
                                                  bandage]

the sun scrapes higher.
the wind dies and the old man
strips the newspaper from his sleeves.   [its]
white leaves and words fall from him   [black]
like winter. *it will come. it will come.*   [and]

he swims on into the sidewalk and shares
breath with all those on the same path,

long or short. to be together is the answer.

lest he forget everything, every night
he returns to the train. every morning
he walks away. this is a ritual. he has   [its ochre]
slowly ground the City into his skin

as vestment. *I am dreaming*, he says.   [in its open mouth]
please. and *help me. anything helps*
in the dream. *it is only a little dream*
and tomorrow I will wake up.   [will flourish]
I have forgotten because I am only
a child and dreaming and tomorrow
I will wake up.

he stumbles and falls from the curb.
someone nudges him, gently, with a shoe.

Catalyst for First Communion #2

an inhalation—

this breath,

then.

we

aspire to

we.

and why

must be

why.

Catalyst for Marriage #1

to embrace the strange
flow of faces in a lunch hour—
eyes, brows, glasses, mouths—   [lips]
therefore, the City makes
a decision that one   [opening]
will be different from before

then. be different from same.

autumn light testifies to
the crisp brim of a fedora,   [to]
chestnut felt and boiled
wool wrapped with black

satin. to honor and obey—

strip off your less necessary
clothes.

find a tryst somewhere metal
and away from the sun.

lean in close with your hand
behind my ear. pronounce your name.

City.

the others kiss, or other and   [form]

if formed for rather, she'd rather
beauty inform uniformity
like birdprints in wet concrete.   [rings]

Catalyst for Communion

reflect just
enough   to puddle the sun—
this basin   so big,
this empty—
so bright—

and also
with you,
my City.

this alone is   an inhalation—
alone again, and—

again?
was the Angel weeping?
where was it?

the desert of morning, back
again.   to take in this breath
she opens behind
herself, then *she*
pries our eyes open. we

have such brave shutters   to shroud
our privilege in—to aspire to.
lashes.   such are the why's

we do not dream any more.
because
of the dreams?   *no, we*
but not we—
a whimper

whipped through wires,   *why,*
a sound wicked through
the darkness   all over
again—

this gift had sounded as if
it had been
keening in it.
someone must be.

Catalyst for Baptism #3

[the cross was replaced]
[with an intersection]

then for a while
every time he got off a train
he was somewhere
he'd never been before.   [an opportunity]
then that stopped, too.

a lavender aurora
blooms over lower
Manhattan.

all the time contained
by bubbles in a flute
of forgotten champagne
is all the time it takes   [to turn]
for snow to disappear
and the moon to draw
a white face close   [or]
enough to kiss. and kissing—
that innocence should demand
such rejection—
and from *Carole*—   [turn away]

the itch stations itself
where it cannot be
reached—   [from belief]

remember whatever you believe.   [in]
within a within it still roams
sidewalks paved with

glass beads—

a belief in electricity—a   [quiet]
source of blue light.

Interlude

do I remember what it was like
to have feet?   [quiet feet]
can I feel them?
do I believe

I still have them—
do I
believe how light rises
through burnished
glass as if to lift the snow—

isn't it grand?
isn't it?   [I remember]

we are being held
but momentarily—

as if springtime,
as if the daffodils
by the bus stop   [snow]
didn't already look
foolish enough—

green clowns—
he is but a being
in this, and foolish for

someone

of gentle mien
and bearing

newsprint
in her fingertips.   *[and]*
                                                      [Carole]
                                 [my City, you're allowed to be]
                                                   [beautiful—]

Catalyst for Confession #1

in determined hat and   [what if]
of indeterminate
age, the man   [an aspect]

on a bicycle
wobbles, both
younger and   [or]
sadder than originally

suspected.

it is cold,
and *I covet*   [an object]

an electric bike.   [implies]
this is one more thing   [a penalty]
to worry about.   [or a penance]

I've spent more
of my time here
peeling oranges
and riding elevators,
or trains,

than I ever thought
I would.

I've spent more—

Catalyst for First Communion #3

offered

we were ever
amen
to everything

amen

creation

estranged

from our own

canticle

celebrate

the sacrifice and
kneel

amen
if not then

then stand

if you can stand

and
exhale

a parable
of ascension
in descent

then
loom

into

faces

and permit faces
to turn

purple

the holy mass of
held breath

Catalyst for Confirmation #4

so she can lean lower and linger   into the sun,
blindness adjusts her hat just so
it brushes his forehead,   and with another
shadow   she relaxes one warm hand onto
his waiting eyes.

loved you, and happily,
there—loved you, you know.   I've always—

the masses sit.   the door hisses—
like breathing under a river.   a river that plummets—
the dog-thought of belief is like that.
the old man breathes.
the line approaches,   and under the East River
it is all back
for a while before the end.   the end of downtown
where their limbs and minds are firm   and starry—

just one more time.

the dog, girl, man, subway—firm—

that they lived—the born, sleeping, risen, dead as the cloudless
sky.
and, in her way,   the City confirms his dream.
almost as if she believed in it,   too. in the sky—

and the City sleeps below herself.   and despite
her dreams of them all   under her arm.
a hat under her arm—

his fists curled and the City tucked
into the width of himself.
the old man pounded his dreams of the girl into
the purple of a world   rolled sideways. he yawned
and the old door hissed back open, just like the lid on
invisible fumes of cheap gin.   and the old man—

he just watched himself sleep, felt his breath escape, and
happily.
he was an old man on a train   and didn't ask why
a forgetful dog   would keep on dreaming of him.

and again old, then, too.   and elsewhere, reinforced,
he seemed to recede, to be bereft,   and he was alone to forget.

or she left, or anyway the City seemed to.   to forget flowers—

at least until
that night. *anyway* was always there   as the third wheel.
concrete and glass cowered once
in a walk-up on the Lower East Side.   at least
together, him and his City,   all together and cozy.
more than once, heaven knew, they clung to a life—

and he found himself on his knees,   more and more
himself.   he married her and he worshipped her.
he chose her,   he had every chance to leave,
but committed—

the City was awful and cruel   but unwittingly
and everything and anyway the City—
a terrible dancer anyway,   what with that filthy scarf—he
knew it was his fault and the girl was probably gone
and he figured it wasn't her fault.   fault—it was less that
than
this word.   so he married the City anyway—*she was so beautiful*—

her again. he was broken then,   and suddenly,   and
true
to everything he ever saw,   but loved—

stupid pounded hat and dogs and garbage and everything.
that beauty could bind him to her   and her scarf—
that terrible and huge and frightening bucket—

he'd marry the City,   *by god,*   *the City herself.*
and every day until she married him,
and every day if not—   he believed
he would be back, and back.

a door hissed open.   the masses stood.

he stopped coming back.

the world will end with
the tolling of bells to the faithless.

the clock's face   with its teardrop tattoos
marked him, marked the calendar,   marked
that he swore   he would come back—

to Washington Square on a Sunday.
and addicts sat still long enough to listen.
and that damned hat and City and dog and any eternal
addicts sitting still   long enough to listen—
on his stone pew,   in his hardest voice he swore to her.
he swore to her as he rounded his back—

under the financial district   and nearing his end—

to proclaim his own faithfulness,
the clacking of wheels intruded   on his sleep. asleep—
his head pounded against the window.   waking into—

the City, he thought,   *always looked pounded.*
in a scarf and a felt hat. purple
to the end, that one,   and beautiful.
once with him   in the open air, she
declined, refined as any other penitent.

he had only asked her to dance,
a triumphal march.   and thus irony. and noontide.
and the hot glare   of the sun on a penny—
and there was no grass, only granite
silhouettes   coloring midday into night.

there you could make out,
like a lightbulb screwed   into every surface,
and pray, everyone on their knees, breathless,
rhythmic.   like a ride out on Coney, like hope
with its feathered tail   waving back and forth.
he held it like   a happy dog tight on its leash—

but she seemed more   afraid,
that Carole, that girl was far more
afraid   than the one he carried forward.

then. to have more than *she*—   one name more—
until when?   maybe he shouldn't have asked her name.

a door opened.   a door hissed closed.

gone. and dirt and heroin lined the unwashed young until
they hit a little corner   that always connected waiting with
4th Street where it defined Washington Square—

a rood screen blocked the light—

as she,   and only as she,   as nameless, as stony—
ended at 4th Street,   the only one he thought of—
velvet curtains and thin hands, only

better?   the old man's image of the girl ended like velvet—
her warm hand on my head.   *what could have been—*
Central Park at noon in November and,   like a grey curtain,
the shade of a linden tree.   *to be a dog in*
nothing there, too.

as a dog I could go on
dreaming and remember.   *if if.*   *if, if.*   *if.*

at the broad gap of Canal, he
wakes—and hangs   in the air for a moment.
below Houston, when the train reaches
below 8th,   nothing is there.
nothing below 14th street.

he remembers   nothing.
ascending, he remembers nothing
in the side tunnels of if and if and if but smoke.
blown and up.   getting larger until burnt sandalwood—

the numbers count out the Bronx until
the old man is sleeping   again
inside of an uptown car,
inside of a black dog   or stale incense—

that dreaming that goes on—

inside of a dog, with
its memories of a local train—

with a whiff of her t-shirt   a door closes.
he coughs into a blue—

that he was young,   then and not
now,   this fills a tin plate.
twine around his finger—
only because—   he tied hemp around—
was because he was young—this—
it would be a mistake to assume it—

molded plastic   and a smell like anesthesia—

some flowers were injections, he knew.
once upon a time,   he did. but not now.
they rose   from meadows. in fact or in seeds—

as if pollen, a puff of yellow smoke
offered a more lasting pew.
in fact,   he could have immolated himself—
any of us could have
chosen our own container   *of sleep*—
like motion, like
he chose a life   in the masses—

he chose his raiment, as much as
walnut.   the color of walnut. the grain,

hard and screwed into the wall.
steel, windows,   and vinyl veneer. something
slides through the doors,   stainless—

the various tines of fiberglass,
not wood,   but something to
trap himself unwittingly on—

the gut strings of the City   that he chose—

to live—

in the consecrated skin that lines her—

that because the man   wrapped himself in these—
or that only because—
to assume it was because   he was old—and given to something
indistinct—   it would be a mistake—

Catalyst for Confirmation #5

is this god's eye
view—   [gravid or]
immune from the diffuse
light of clouds,   [innocuous]
or falling?   [the sky]
the hope to
construct
a tower tall   [appeals]
enough to push back
the sunset into
the infinite
meniscus of the sea.   [more or]
a river or the coastline   [less]
between coastlines.

or maybe the sun
comes up. it traces

a seam
of hot iron along the   [tempered]
limits of the tower built.
the red lights go out

one by
one, lower and   [into]

lower,
like torches hurled into the   [immutable]
embrace of the Hudson.
so begins a litany of praise—
the buildings   [blue]

are beautiful.

all the little trees
are green as velvet couches.

as the sun soars
higher
the cardinals start
to wallow in scarlet.

Catalyst for Baptism #4

beautiful,
we're allowed to be—
and Carole, too—
City   in her fingertips.

newsprint collects,
bearing someone
of gentle mien—
someone gentle,   someone
mine
in this life,   and foolish for it.
we are being

green clowns—
foolish enough before—and
didn't we already look it
by the bus stop   in the snow.

as if the narcissus—
as if springtime,
but   momentarily—

glass lifts the snow—
through burnished
light, it rises.
do I believe   in melting?

can I feel the snow   wake into heat?
does the sublime have feet? quiet feet—
do I remember what it was like?

a source of blue light,
a belief in electricity—   a quiet

I will say

prayed along glass beads—

I do not want this anymore.
within a within the quiet   still roams.

remember what you believe.
what you reached for—   out of belief.

and from Carole—*turn away.*
from the City,   such rejection—
that innocence should demand
so much and offer
only enough to kiss.   and kissing—

a face   to disappear in
is all it takes to turn

forgotten.
all the time contained
by Manhattan.

Manhattan bloomed over lowered
lavender twigs,   an aurora then—

that stopped, too.

he'd never been an opportunity before.

but with Carole   he was somewhere
every time he got off a train.

and for a while,
with an intersection,

his cross was replaced.

Catalyst for Marriage #2

rings

form

as

open
lips

Catalyst for Baptism #5

his City wore her violet hat   [like a kiss]
like a still-panting
animal, but it was nothing—   [this wind]
she said, *it's nothing*—
when measured against the cold.
like faces when crushed against
faces, the wind left   [a knocking sound and]
no room for breath.
her eyes spilled down   [heavier than lashes]
in the last tears   [there was nothing heavier]
they had to offer.

so like a winter park,
the park in winter

took them, gladly.
it could not
give them back
any more

than it could forgive.

nor did the dirt
offer any

sign of gratitude.   [nothing]

for a little penance
the old man sat for years
while the bluegrass grew.
for forgetting.

he willed it
blue—
and *bluer—yes.*
yes, that would have made
my son happy.

that would have made us all
happy.
that would have made us all—

Catalyst for Confirmation #6

I could get used
to these—

wings

emerge,   then fly—
in reversal, rectangles of white
already popped into breath—

reflections on shadow and night—
the—
morning,   a breath of light
squirms against glass,
a building's east side—
winks   from a third-floor window,
a photographer's strobe—

one two three—

breath shines between bricks.

now   it has gone from me.
but, if truly gone,
I should have seen it go—

no—   his own voice, now, certain—   *I can feel it*
passing—

he can feel   his breath and this
now, this when, this end
when stars grow   blue behind eyelids
into an   older, longer now—

furled
by invitation—

bring the night in   from itself.
offer comfort   to the face of wind—

I forgive it for all its winter—
the cruelty in trying

to face the wind.
a screen of marled wool rips
from where it shielded
his eyes—   then the sky is there—

decisive—

the old man   will place himself in it.
or not. he sees
the altar laid out beneath him.

he sees he will be a meal
for time.   the altar waits in soon.
any of us could see it—

the inevitable, too, is of whether.
and regardless,   into it
the sun disappears— in steam
or girders or ribs.

chests—   ripple,

and fall—

the old man—

see there,   a glimmer on the rise.

Catalyst for Extreme Unction #2

this too

will flourish

and its open mouth

its ochre

and
black
its hope

without a bandage

a sore

flowers
raw

in bloom

bed
broken

life in
the remnants of

Catalyst for Confession #2

the old man

turns away.

the dimension of *them*—
so many of *them*—

one could almost step into,   [the masses]
but then only almost

a face

made clearer in relief.

struggling against—
dealing with—
his long life
becomes

prepositional.
by, on, beside,
alongside, beneath, under,
and only occasionally
inside.

Catalyst for Baptism #6

is a City ever
so much
as in leaving?
or, like exhaled
breath, does it
become geography—

as paper
cutouts glued
to a blue wall—

a sheer victim of mere

or other-
wise dismissed.

is this a willing blindness, or

has the old man
truly
erased into the rain?

Catalyst for Confirmation #7

there, in the rise
and fall—
chests—   [a ripple]
of girders and ribs   [in steam]

the sun disappears—
regardless
of whether
any humans see it.

a catalyst
or not?

the old man places his   [ripped]
hand over his eyes—
a screen of marled wool
to face the wind,
a small comfort in the face of wind

allows

the night in.   [from itself]
an invitation—   [and]
the furled
flag of a particular now,
when stars collide behind eyelids—
stationed in

this now, this

when.
he can feel the breath
passing—
his own—*I can feel it.*

I could see it,
but   [gone]
now it has gone from me.

Catalyst for Confirmation #8

the

shadow and night—
that already pops—   [into breath]

rectangles of white
emerge, then fly by
on celluloid

wings.
I could get used to these
incendiary things.

Baptism

of another winter gone—
mud is the memory of
snow—

like gravestones or
how a gull sleeps on the sea.

the soft sun.

he closes his eyes—
the dwindling wind—
a warm day in February—
quiet as a narcissus
beginning to bloom. for once,

[a five-year-old boy in]
[his memory or his]
[astronaut suit]
[imagine]
[he danced]

the old man floats
on a pleasant dream.   [on the uptown train]
brief as
the sky—   [until scolded]
and too quickly
closed   [into stillness]
before a storm—

there was a child, then gone.

Catalyst for Confirmation #9

sitting in a bare locust tree
sometimes the City can only   be

a memory
apprehended—
in reverse,

a reflection
versed in the vagaries
of its own glass.

structures propagate   in structures,
conspire
to keep the sun out,

as three statues without
memories   or torsos might.

to   swallow their words,
a taxi arrives.
its brake lights
approach a brownstone
through the rain.

light   reaches
out   to him
like a draft
through   an open
                  door.

Catalyst for Extreme Unction #3

a vacuum lingers
where his son once was.
this change in pressure
manifests itself as   [noise]
a popping of the ears—
from tunnel to station,   [is the]
widening.

these symptoms could be   [first]
softened simply
by chewing gum.

or death.
in the parking lot
later, a change
in pressure also

manifests itself
as an unfolded pigeon—   [warning that]
a wheel and feathers leave
a chest, soon to be a carcass.
widening.   [we receive]

interestingly, these
symptoms, too—they could be
softened by chewing gum—

a pink mass to plug a sucking
wound.

Catalyst for Ordination #3

the witnesses begged for
grace

before he shattered

across the ground

returning
before

his return

they
begged for

pilgrims
father and child

of holy
lines
both

in the cathedral
and

outside

Catalyst for Marriage #3

like birdprints,   wet concrete wrings
beauty from sand to inform uniformity.

and, if formed for rather,   *I'd rather*
another kiss—   *forms*

behind his ear.   *I'd rather it pronounced her name.*
leaned in close with her hand,   *just so,*

away from the sun.
let's find a tryst somewhere metal.

clothes—
strip off your less necessary

satin.   *then honor. then obey.*
wool wrapped over black memories

and eggplant silk, felt and boiled—
her lingerie   like the crisp brim of a fedora—

autumn light testified to this.
then be different from same. to

be different from before,
therefore one must   make a decision that one's

eyes, brows, glasses, mouths—   open—
to let—to let one's lips

trace the lines of another's face   for one hour—
if only to embrace the strange.

Eucharist

without—

a swaying figure, or
a light to answer—

how could he know?   [survival]

how could he
discern the subtle
difference between twisting

and writhing—

the possibilities of privacy—

without
remembering her face?   [is this a question]

he held a tender   [unanswered]
flame in his hand,
that expression on
her face,

her wind,

breathing so
that breath should literally become fire—
and him,   [by]

watching the news-
paper closely,
it began to curl.

he read the black
print. the heat
impressed despite the jealous
wind. and jealous of   [respiration]

the wind, the fire, too,
leapt into nothing.
carbon dioxide, water,   [breath]

a sack for wind—   [binds itself]
he exhaled.
he tried again.

determined, he
laced a cradle   [to breath]
with the bones of

his hands—*here*—
lick my hands. this world's dirt is in them,
he said, *you have your place*
now, to grow. I know—   [and]
I know you're hungry, too.
eat. and grow into—   [finally]
myself. fire tethers itself to paper.   [to ash]

the way warm air and sound
transubstantiate—

the escape

of life into speech.
words. and words, and *Carole.*
speaking or writing,

how miserable a person or
a fire would be—
chewing at a table—like this me was—
I remember this me,

this many-legged language machine.
now how blessed in silence.
this many-breathed engine of
begging and belief. these hands.

this burning page—this

relic
of my childhood

faith in gibberish—
air and fire.

Catalyst for Confession #3

[disappointment begins with]

expectation—

behind   [a thin gap]

glass looks much fancier than it is—   [for]

the crack penetrates the panes   [expectations]
where the cold scrabbles in
to get eaten by steel tables—   [to fall through]

a catalog of—

shiver—
his shoulders first, then his chin.

drink—
the drinks that have soured.
old coffee. the winter air.
night.

pity—
the black dog chained
to a post outside the coffee shop.

Catalyst for Extreme Unction #4

City,
when I listen
I listen to hear—   [you]

to be there for you

if you unravel.
but you never do.
you breathe—   [sleep]
and sometimes hold   [or you hold onto]
my breath—I

place
my why—my left

hand cross-wise   [my breath]
on your chest,
unrivaled,

I alone revel in
its rise.

we agree not to
reveal to each other
we're dying.
we agree not to mention our son.

we agree not to talk about the fact

it's winter again.
we both hear the wind—   [for later]
it creeps in
under blankets of dark.   [at night]
it creeps in around panes.

Communion

the previous glimpse
was a windshield.
framed in chrome.

the gift sounded like   [the why]
someone   [must be]
keening in.

the darkness all over again—   [the]
sound wicked like
whipped wires,   [why]

a whimper
but not
a dream. no   [we]

because

we do not dream any more.
this is
the privilege: to   [aspire to]

have shutters to
pry our eyes
open behind,   [then]

again to take in   [this breath]
the narrow desert of morning.

where was it
the Black Angel was weeping
again?   [I must be]

alone again, and
this alone is—   [an inhalation]

with you,
and also with you—

so bright,
this empty
basin big
enough
to puddle the sun.

First Communion

a sacrament,   [the holy mass of]
the masses
clad in sacred   [purple]
raiment, the holy robe
of trust—take this air,
each of you, and breathe
it. it is the breath   [and faces]
of your own body.
take this water, each
of you. it is   [faces]
the flesh of your flesh.
we are the sea, made   [into]
flesh. we share such that
the other may be other
than the other. the   [gloaming]
masses multiply
with masses. like the paupers' gowns

of supplicants, we are weft
and warp of faith—   [if you can stand]
this air, know it has been breathed and may
be breathed again.   [then stand]
this City, it has swallowed
before, and will again. and amen.
if we are lucky, we grow
from the same ground our grandparents
are buried in. if not, then we find a way
to live on the bones of strangers.   [if not, then]
the first bite is hard, but   [kneel]
they say it gets easier after that.

the chewing
grows more comfortable with time.   [sacrifice, and]

less than aimless, and more.
the masses—   [celebrate]
when I arrive, the masses
put on their best clothes
and walk out—the others
are clad in black, too, and   [these penultimate canticles]
only grow more
resplendent on the sidewalks.
onyx. obsidian. ebony. rarity.

and beautiful in the
way that ostrich plumes
on the foreheads of horses are
beautiful. we dye the world
black in the presence of the living.   [of our own]

we wake. we eat to honor our dead.
we feast on our dead selves.
so they walk out and straight
up Thompson, between the black
Lincolns slick with rain,
between the yellow cabs, handsome,
to a glass door, wet linoleum,
and fluorescent wash. steam clings to
red vinyl chairs and chrome.   [strange]
they pray. they pray to each
other, to Spring Street, to Famous Ben's—
please, they pray. please

give us old love and thin napkins.
give us a slice fat enough to roll

and the opulence of orange   [and social]
grease-stains on paper plates.
give us all this, please,   [creation]
they pray, and we will honor it.

give us someone to sit next to   [amen]
at this table   [amen]
and we will offer up our lives.
we will give away our breath.   [amen]

anyone might have. the masses did.

I did the same. I prayed.   [to everything]
and the feast was so hot.   [we were ever]
it blistered my throat.
but I ate. I ate it all. all that was,   [offered]
was, in that moment, love.

[as if to exit.
as if a departure, rather
than an arrival—
I am going, as if to mass,
but I shall return.
and it shall be as if

I never left. the City shall be
as if none of us ever meant to. as if we
never left it. it shall persist.
it shall resist departure,
passively—which is to say, as if
it sits. as if it waits for rupture—
as if to exit. all those far away fields of wheat
will fall to fallow then. and then we will gather them in
as if to celebrate a harvest. as if to break
bread. as if breaking bread were as if.

the same as. as if an exit.
take this. take this, Arnim, my son, and eat.
as if to not eat would be the same as
as if to not remember you.]

Catalyst for Extreme Unction #5

anticipating a certain sort of darkness,   [the lost youth]
a long line of human forms and
the nerve roots of trees
protrude from the poor   [stamped]
soil from which they were torn.
concrete holes. in particular, this
subway station is just one more entrance to
the underworld. it stops where   [the mud]
words of Whitman kiss
forlorn commuters goodbye.

in silence in dreams' projections—   [from]

sometimes they descend,
smoothly sliding, without a hitch, and   [their feet]
sometimes—especially when rain pelts
down—the steps bind them, then lurch
to a halt. they say this type of
entrance is the worst, by far,   [the blood pools]
when escape is needed most
the escalators fail and frantic
people trample over each other   [in cracks]
vainly climbing for breath.   [in steel]

Whitman. the name is deeply etched.
no one has scrawled Eckert in the cracks—
no one painted the shape of his mouth
black. in particular, this abyss

is a circle,   [to be collected]
lest we forget circles are where

the system most often fails.   [in]
a snowflake, it flutters down   [air]
to reach the old man's outstretched
hand before it melts.

Confirmation

he
determined,
then,
he would stay here   [to pray]
as breath or at least
as a question—

if,
this *if*—

if—

what if—
a question

is engrossing, enough
to fill a life-

time

but, the answer
is unbearably

dull—

Ordination

just let the building kiss him,   they begged.
so the City blessed him before   he shattered
the park's slats and benches,   then ground
the street itself   through him—

I will tug the wind through it all;
I will whistle through the fall.
I am returning.   *eat me whole*

before a grey wing and the wind   *do;*
and make me beautiful, too.
like blue tendons and sky,   *bless me.*

his arms strained backwards into tall—
so beautiful,   he whispered as the
taxis, the umbrellas,   and the masses returned for him—
the wires that competed with wires, the
garbage, the antennas, the ropes,
the trees, the maples,   the bees, the concrete, the
flowers,   the poor huddled pigeons
in their fear.   their black talons begged for
stones, bricks, and steel. the
rivers, the water towers, the pilgrims

fell down—   the glass, the walls, the
narrow world   and all he saw on the way—
this earth   and these other birds, he felt
a wordless call   to tell them all about
hunger,   this hunger for a hard
falcon's perspective—life in death, of holiness

at the last—   that he would serve
for the wind.   it was decided, then,
his path would become a vertical line—
like gemstones   or sunlight

falling through an angels' hair.
he drafted the curve of gravity, a
screen   to divide a building from the sky.
past guards and at last
over the rude railing—
out of the elevator,   past the drowsy
altitude   where winter does what it will—
a white floor.   the sun was low as he sprinted—
November 3rd and the 103rd tier.
it was the Great Depression,   they said.
whether it was morning or not,   it was the cathedral.

the same as feathers
of the Bible,   it would have ended.
if Icarus were given leaves,
one each for his widening eyes, they said
the leaves   would have been religious
medallions from his pockets,   rough as a
prayer book   in his two calloused hands,
and heavy enough to tip him past
enough. he went.   he went outside as
Frederick Eckert,   who, as Frederick Eckert,
was 32, free, and difficult to be.   in the end,
it was his own causality   that stopped him,
and not the ground.
he went happily to nothing.

Confession

the old man wakes
to unexpected
sunlight—tries to blink into

life—
is that you
that away from sound—

a breath—
Carole? a whisper—

Arnim?
unseen throughout
the park crawls

an undulate wail—
they could just be playing

how at a distance   [both]
screams sound—   [potentially innocent]

just like a torrent
of wind torn

through the crack in a wall.

distinguished or indistinguishable.

how up close—
they are.   [and]

was I
a question for another time—

how broken their syntax
is, but not irretrievably so.

how the morning's frost
on a lamp post

scrapes   [potential]
away just like his
memory—   [of innocence]

at best
I offered little ease—

how a memory of another
pleased—how the closing door
of a pleasant dream didn't—

Marriage

the older the man gets
the more he wants his last words

to be,   *I love you.*

and the more he says
them   to strangers—
nameless,   and these words,
the more to strangers—

                              I've always loved you.

and the more hopefully—

Extreme Unction

someone nudges him,   gently, with a shoe.
he stumbles and falls from the curb.
I will be a child   and tomorrow I will wake up.
I have forgotten because I am only myself,
and tomorrow I will wake up   and flourish
without the dream.   it is only a little dream.
please.   and help me. anything helps.
   I am only dreaming, he says.

and the dream's open mouth
slowly grinds the City into his skin.
he walks away into the dream—this is a ritual; he has its ochre.
he returns for the train   every morning
lest he forget everything,   every night
long or short.   to be together is the answer.
to breathe   with all those on the same path;
swim on into the sidewalk   and share
like winter.   *it will come. it will come.* and
white leaves and words will fall from him.

the old man strips the black newspaper from his sleeves.
the sun scrapes higher.   the wind dies and
he tries to remember his home,
and can't without the bandage
of the subway   that will take him there.
too, he thinks of the one long bottle of forgiven
while he dreams.   the bottle is a ticket
and with it he will be.   forgiven. it's
his ticket out, he knows.   at the bottom of every
offered palm it returns to pay for   the next sorrow—

the next dirty quarter that only appears in
his dream anymore.   it is a bad dream—and a sore.
take it, he thinks. *take me.* he doesn't need or want a
name   when it comes time to hand this story to the City.
the last laced dregs of his sanity—   he forgets his,
always punctuated with profanity   and fear, anyway,
their chain of causation.   so his interior narration
flowers into waiting   again.   he forgets the improbable
marking of time he has begun. raw
alms arrive   outside the station. or don't. and without
these he returns   to the slow digestion
inside and the dreaming.   this realization bores in—

if not for the wind it might still be
Sunday, or clouds—   if not for the wind.
the bloom of daylight gnaws at something
that might have been hiding.
under the blanket of his dream,
the old man treads water drawn
from the boards of his Grand Terminal pew.
he has nowhere better—
he forgives them for this.

the masses beneath the rain   walk a little cleaner.

beneath the old man,   the City goes on dreaming.
grease— in the dream, a memory of food.
in a bed he would be as trapped as a plate, as coated.

a few puddles remain,   shriveling, as storms
flow past with other trash and mistakes
broken off cast-iron grates.   and the rain
is a clamshell—it snaps.   and the plate snags. bars

build him a paper-plate house and a polystyrene
life in a storm drain,   a medium for swimming.

last night's downpours gurgle.
motor oil bathes the remnants of his face.

Recessional

Frederick Eckert breathed
a little more and only
ashamed until   he became air.

and then stopped.   then not alone in if—
and if to breathe,
ultimately   to stop.

and if to step,   wreathed
in sky ultimately, if only
a millimeter, into   clear air

to breathe what if.   to say—
and what if to hold is to never
reach,   a never to breathe, to

speak *I have found you*
here, to exhale *I have*
always loved you,   a never

to find ground again. in this City,
flight would be the same as if
falling was a prayer   hung and thus—

eternal.
if he became
          air   and belief

came home to sing to him,
to grief,   he would be the same
as if.   as if wings and lungs were.

PART 3: EPILOGUE

February 17, 2013

under the City,
inside the increasing
darkness and
pressure   of a dream—
a narrative shears.

the train   stops—

the doors open with an *if*—

if the wet bellows
freeze—

if a crystal should
form—

if the black dog wakes up with

a hope for this old man's
doom   to change,
that the next   meager
liturgy would then be more
human.   or less.

Acknowledgments

The author wishes to thank the editors of *Otoliths, Viator, Paris Lit Up, Bear Review* and *E-Ratio*, who saw fit to publish many of the poems in this book. Thank you for your faith and support.

This book was a long time coming. It never would have happened without the consultation and engagement of Elizabeth Robinson, Jennifer Phelps, Richard Schwass and Jenny Henry. Thank you, one and all. You were there every step of the way. You're lovely.

Photo: Sarah Suzor

Travis Cebula lives in Colorado with his wife and trusty dogs, where he writes, edits, photographs and teaches creative writing. He is the author of six full-length collections of poetry, including *Dangerous Things to Please a Girl*, a sequence of Parisian poetry, and *After the Fox*, a collaboration with Sarah Suzor, available now from Black Lawrence Press. He is also a member of the writing faculty at Left Bank Writers Retreat in Paris, France, a Pavel Srut Fellow, a finalist, an honorable mention, several rejections and generally tries to be a nice guy—which offers him a few excuses. On most days, you can find him somewhere between the margins. On some days, you can't.